reflecting mercury

Dreaming Shakespeare's Sonnets

by
Raficq Abdulla

**Panarc
International**

Published by
Panarc International 2016

Copyright © Raficq Abdulla, 2016

First Edition

The author asserts the moral right
under the Copyright, Designs and Patents Act 1988
to be identified as the author of this work.

All rights reserved. No part of this publication may be
reproduced, stored in a retrieval system or transmitted,
in any form or by any means without the prior consent
of the author, nor be otherwise circulated in any form of
binding or cover other than that in which it is published
and without a similar condition being imposed on the
subsequent purchaser.

www.panarcpublishing.com
Panarc International Ltd
www.panarc.com

ISBN : 978-0-9931103-3-7
Epub:: 978-0-9931103-4-4
Kindle: 978-0-9931103-5-1

Cover design and typesetting by
Chandler Book Design

Printed in the United Kingdom
by Ingram Sparks

DEDICATION

I dedicate this book to the fickle present which
tantalises and eludes us always.

ACKNOWLEDGMENTS

I thank Marianne and Adam for their constant moral
support, and Salim Janmohamed and Mohamed
Keshavjee for their vital practical help without which
this book would not have seen the light of day.

INTRODUCTION

*"cette hésitation prolongée entre
le son et le sens"*

PAUL VALÉRY

Shakespeare's sonnets have always been an enigma to me – I love his plays for their language, for their rich, sometimes devastatingly acute imagery, for their strong narrative drive and characterization, and finally for their wit, depth and wisdom – but the sonnets were, and perhaps remain, a cul-de-sac for me. I was bound, imprisoned as it were, in a fog of incomprehension. I did not want to "study" the sonnets, read *about* them, learn from the ratifying rhetoric of sagacious scholars and professing academics presenting ostensive ways on how to "read" them thus weaving speculative fabrics of settled meanings and necessary orthodoxies of account. I did not want to imbibe the constructions of others to lead me into the fascinating labyrinth of relationships the sonnets construct. I wanted to encounter them - their music - personally, nakedly, and yet, each time I tried to read them, I felt that I simply did not get under their mercurial surface literally and metaphorically. I could not pin down their brilliant show.

I decided that rather than read them yet again and reach an impasse, I would "converse" with them – sonnet to sonnet – I would engage with Shakespeare obliquely, as if we were sitting together with a convivial glass in hand, in a quiet corner - he having taken a break from his busy life at the Globe and me, rising from my poetic stupor. I would reflect upon, and reflect his divining verse which turns about the covert stations of love, yearning, dread and loss that afflict us all one way or another; perhaps to contradict it, perhaps to dance with its raptures of creation, perhaps to play with it in imaginative encounter, and thus approach these poems with the charmed serendipity of close conversation where meaningful words come to mind, spontaneously. I might then begin to reach below the skin of ambiguities and subtleties of his poetry. By this process of intuitive exchange of precarious realities, Shakespeare, in a sense, would become my analyst and I his willing analysand, and vice-versa, by the occult practice of listening attentively with an open heart to his words, which, in time, might become necessary to me.

And so I began this personal exploration of these marvellous poems. Though, in a sense I still do not comprehend them if by that word we mean possession or ownership. They are not simply gloss but the epitome of living and loving in a transient world of perennial departures. Relating thus to the sonnets has taught me what Wordsworth, in his Preface to the *Lyrical Ballads*, calls "…the grand elementary principle of pleasure".

So I stopped trying to understand the poems and in the place of this seemingly impossible task, I decided to practise the pleasure of *hearing* them for their music – their ignited, contrapuntal energy of sound and rhythm - with a mimetic, ear rather than construe them for their meaning which remains, for me, tantalizing but elusive. Yet I wanted to be acquainted, to get to know them, to converse with them as one does with friendly but obscure strangers, to exchange ideas with them, and even to argue with them about beauty's beguiling deceptions that draw on misguided and fatal loyalties making memory intensely desirable and the reason to live on. The craft of poetry eludes me. I am not a good reader of poetry in that I cannot readily explicate a poem, recognize its structure and intention or intentions, and so on. I read simply, and as I read I struggle to recognize a poem and thus my liminal self. Hence, I tend to read with my ears rather than with my eyes. And so I have learnt to *hear* the sonnets, to receive the hermetic and fecund layers of meaning beneath the tapestry of sound and so, in turn, to echo them, discover them and hopefully, replenish them for our time. I hope in this book I have been able to listen out for, and listen into the marveling, interlacing and intimate lines of love and loss, the throb of disappointment and death, the masochistic ironies of betrayed love, that Shakespeare so elegantly and obsessively plays into being in his sonnets.

Raficq Abdulla © 2016

1

With your lines you might deceive posterity of me
But ask not to add myself to make a three
From you and me thus take possession of you
To second me, so by eye, from smile, or through
Turn of phrase, familiar cough or temper, raise
Hopes of dilute immortality; you would phase
Me into you so my own decease is mere deception
Or so you like to think, others read, but their reception
Is misconstrued, I cannot repeat myself nor
Can you for me, we are conceived not to store
Our fates but to expend, we are *passim*, acute
Mortality for eating time, our becoming is moot,
We go from dark to dark travelling light between,
Write as you will, but when we die, we die never to be seen.

When two score winters do thee keep
Your beauty unwritten with time, you weep
Pathos that shrouds with tears your eyes
To declare memory blind, when your ties
To youthful pleasure are severed, cut loose,
You shall be asked: Where's your beauty? No use
Wagering it with your eyes where once your soul
Resided and soft-spoken desire inscribed the roll
Of your hips, your glowing body's pivot; if only
You could mirror yourself with child, lonely
Age will not rescind you, for you shall return
With youth pricked with familiar talents, surely burn
The candle at both ends if you must, yet you'll travel again
From this issue afresh and make youth your eternal refrain.

If not pleasure let pain make a speculator of you,
Look in the placid mirror, toward the shaded glass
You see a miracle you take for granted; you're too
Complaisant with the number left to you, years will pass,
Your muscle and skin shall inherit the dust of time
To become, in your sun year's decline, themselves ashes;
You are prime now, engendered with beauty that's sublime
To your lover's eye, today your becoming grace splashes
All who swim near to you, yet you are only one,
Alone your floating beauty shall time's siege forfeit;
You have but one passage to enter, no girl will shun
The mien of your body and soul; you must see fit
To act as nature would have you do to multiply,
So name your issue thus your beauty to exemplify.

You squander this beauty loaned to you
Restoring yourself with the argent that lies
In your perfect mirror-image repeats; true
Your are beauty's beauty now, but you try
Nature's bounty not yours to hoard; you accrue
No new capital with your miserly disregard,
But use your beauty so scarcely deployed, few
Shall witness its shine when you are taken hard
And cold from time into shaded eternity: the spend
Of your beauty's energy is pledged with self-deceit,
You lease yourself to selfish pleasure, bend
Your lover to your will with pleasant conceit,
But your castrate beauty shall fade without issue,
Your passing shall die itself, and none shall miss you.

Restless time baits the seasons to a loop,
Summer to autumn runs to winter stoops.
So these hours where you're fairly framed
Are detached from booted spring, they claim
No loyalty to the infinite moment's bliss
Where risen sap is sweetened with a lover's kiss.
Winter's desiccated touch is our common fate
When beauty is disowned, the several years dislocate
All ambitious prime, make bastard of pedigree hope,
Marrow turned to lead, skin made rough as rope
Now summer's hale welcome resorts to autumn's fare;
Life turns sober, resolves to roots that nurse and care
For its rebirth when the cycle moves round again,
Winter marches on, spring returns with beauty in train.

Make from the seasons' sphere your season's ear
To fuse your energy's youth; yet look ahead, fear
Winter's coming rages, reform your sun distilled
From summer's lease which like airy music filled
Your listening with murmur of soft viols' trace
In enclosing sighs that keep your will in place,
And plant a new paradise for your springing race.
Leave not your beauty in need, you are nature's face,
You have your fate to declare, invest your capital
Where interest may yield a tenfold share hospitable
In time so time might you pare without beauty's loss.
Thus take you death in hand, discard your self-denial
Come alive when you recede from winter's harsh trials,
Let this winter passing be your breathing beauty's gloss.

Eyes fretful of staining night open to the rising sun,
A fresh orient miracle that cuts with horizon's knife
They unwittingly serve as night now they shun.
This escalating, redemptive god essential to life
Receives the homage due from everyone;
Inch by inch its *aubade* rises to a zenith point
Reeling back the day, then youth's hypocrite meridian
Is reached that strokes the fawning gaze, anoints
From a parabola of streaming light, then time is past
With nothing to look forward but hopeless dying,
The wear and tear of body and soul flying half-mast,
Thus once-serving eyes turn away, give themselves to lying
About your true estate that lingers in the finite afternoon,
Replace yourself or death shall remove all trace of you too soon.

A single dying note resounds like a tolling bell,
A single sighing prospect travels one way to hell.
But two marrying notes, now they may issue three!
Love's dialectic jumps from single combat to harmony.
Do not solely pluck yourself when you're allowed
A greater sound to create; infertile solitude disavowed
By all teasing posterity is only to be shunned;
In pleasure lies the key, share yourself with it, be stunned
To such a degree, your rebel beauty ripples from the core,
So spread yourself as music spreads from silence's score.
Receive in duplicate what is truly yours to create gladly,
Breathe out your body's song with the joy that madly
Craves to join its mate, by this union bring true order
To your beauty, revive your beloved, and so reward her.

What are you afraid of? To love, to marry
Is not without heartache and conscripted loss;
To marry is to join pleasure with risk, to carry
The advantage of another's joy you don't toss
Like a forgotten coin to a beggar in the street,
For that is your employment, the stone of change,
Fear not that you depreciate if you should meet
The woman who would join with you and derange
With pitching desire; for should you die alone
Without printing a second impression of your face
The world will mourn you a while but you shall be bone
Of grief, dry and soon forgotten, at table an empty place;
To keep desire intact is to steal yourself, you surely fail
Thus to declare your beauty which fades without entail.

10

Your apparent love is unreliable, burning salt
That rubs the wounds of the many who love you.
You are love's actor, a player of devious parts, halt
At nothing you derogate for your vanity's gain; few
Things you love so indulgently as yourself, or hate,
For love and hate are affiliate cousins whose loyalties hold
A family of vipers to make ruin with; you dictate
A familiar story when you disdain those who are sold
On your unwitting charm desire develops, their love
Relates new torments of discouragement; poles apart
They appear blasphemous to your cruelty that's above
The longing which afflicts true lovers who cannot depart
Making insanity of reasonable discourse; they love your soul,
They would be the mirror of posterity your beauty to enrol.

As soon as you die, as soon you live again
In a million compliant parts that fly and shoot out
From you, you give yourself a chance to rein
In time's deprivation of your beauty, your scouts
Seek sanctuary, where one might prosper, you increase;
Without this native ecstasy, you and the world be closed,
All joy and hungry expectation, all hope, would cease.
There are enough ugly creatures, time's puppets, to dispose.
No, you must stay and prevail, replenish your store,
Enter then and be on your mettle, prepare to perform
Nature's symmetry as you should, you are nature's pledge more
Than any other who aspects your act, so yourself reform
Anew, stamp the seal that clement nature breeds in you,
Wax yourself, marshal your genius, brand your new issue.

We are sepulchered, to be shaded with coming age
When unwitting youth our bending season does presage;
Nothing keeps so well as time you see; not rose
Nor even oak banked with insolent leaves, not the hair
Of a girl in her prime that is satin, nor would you depose
Your proper purpose thus to beauty's fickle order; share
Your summer's spring into autumn's rage if you must, manic
The hallowed boiling, fraught the cooling of the blood,
You are ruined by aging reason's deploying panic;
Joints grows dense, memory rescinds, sinks in the mud
Of your cold agonies, your sweated fears. You shall travel
As a bit player in time's cast, the play of your speech unravel,
It shall be of no avail against the fatal hour - you are waste
Unless you exceed yourself from rusting time's final embrace.

13

To be yourself, to suppose your beauty true
Is a conceit to disturb your complacency, say
The word but do not trust your own through
The miscellany of your view of what is, or may
Be if imagination were a foil; you resemble
Your banking antecedent susceptible enough to find
A posterity for himself loving you, he didn't dissemble
But realised his face in your loan, so would you bind
Your errant self lent to you by time, you make
A new world, issue new currency fresh to exchange
Yourself from surcease, a rising sun that takes
For granted the appreciating day; but range
Your unthrifty eye against the coming end, supply
A succeeding self, let loose your life before you die.

I do not process the preening stars, read the future good
Or hell, bode the rising east with fortune's feast or plague,
Nor can I speculate how each rounded minute should
Break out of its shell to newly bear its element with vague
But compulsive words shunning clarity; I am dusty with advice
For my peers' satisfaction, seeing no future I can tell
From stars in their celestial prime, they glitter a price
Too dear for my fretting wit not sure enough in the well
Of my being to read a fruitful heaven there; but from your eyes
I reach a knowledge that tempts me with their truant art,
From these stars of yours truth and beauty figure and rise
If you would free them to enterprise from your starry chart.
Or I am bound to make a prophecy accruing for your fire,
When it dies, contracted truth and beauty shall duly expire.

A Digression

I am no seer who reads the stars,
Plucks mystery from their nightly eyes.
Yet I am briefed by arcana that mar,
Plunder the soul's expanse - light which flies
To prophecy impelled by good and evil luck.
I cannot see so far to plagues, nor famines construe;
To serve such angry masters who augur and pluck
The eye of courage, I know not nor ever knew.
I am no pander, nor princes' soiled professional
Practised in the art, a predicating preacher, dressed
In flattery which oils God in the confessional;
Truth plunders the spirit that parks itself in flesh,
I am a professor of the nuance of your gaze, blessed
With doubtful grace enough to feel you change, mesh
With your beauty's title to christen your face
Not your own but pinned to time and place.

My eye absorbs the fleeting moment's perfection
From everything which grows, passing state to state
Knowing no resting place, like air in convection
Rising first than falling back, receipt of earth that waits
To absolve all forms to their last estate, a charge
Of dust that dances in the spectacle of stars.
We are ornaments, first shine with time at large
Dazzling ourselves with our savage health on par
With gods ingrained in our innocence, then dull
We grow in eye, laggard in limb, our skin turns to hide,
We're eclipsed by other rising earths' insolence full
Of new adjournments hoping against time's dark tide.
You too are overcome, your sequestered beauty fades,
Grafts its season in this report's timely light and shade.

16

But why do you not spring into raging war
Against time's tyranny? You can make more
Of yourself than these placid signs can do
Even held to view a thousand years hence.
You are rich with youth and beauty few
Can compete, women are yours to have; don't fence
With your shadow that daily grows to hold over
Your darting virtue, you are fortunate with a surfeit
To spend, but you must act to end the cover
Of your selfishness, replace this tepid counterfeit
With real spending from your succeeding press,
So your living face may, with impressive show
Bow out as it must when you reach your time's excess,
Your traces then shall reconcile you to its deleting flow.

My words are poor judges that helpless lie
When passing sentence on your beauty, the light
Of your eyes escape my sound that does not fly
To heights sufficient not to demean with their flight.
Heaven hides your many parts that beauty strikes
With desire's spark that none can speak of or write
But only savour from the compass of their being,
This is experience to be felt in silence without seeing.
Who will believe my sentences when you're gone?
Your present eyes made absent without time borne
To the shallow grave of words that can only tell?
You can remedy yourself with another, time doesn't quell
But passes over the projected legacy of your inherited seed,
Then may you commend yourself not in word but in deed.

18

How can a summer's day compare with you?
It is heavy sun or louring cloud, rain
In the offing; you're airy presence and touch, a cue
For greater things and states to come, both pain
And joy, the rub of pleasure no mere day conceives.
Your beauty *aspires* and points the way
To Arcadian seasons of the mind where we perceive
Our gorgeous fantasies, shining attire on display.
Your summer's ever-rising zenith shall never cease
Nor be pocketed by death's felony, its sly approach;
You are here in your own sure way, you are leased
To timely lines which time's business reproach.
So long as some shall read and love shall see
So blind is death as you are phrased by me.

Time you accident's darling, black night
Your flag, you dance and devour, reduce
All creatures thrown to the elements, your sight
Is death, empty winds in blind corners produce
Your song, toothless the tiger, the phoenix burnt,
The rusted lock, the rotting elm, the dying light
In widowed eyes, the stiffening legacy learnt
Through sorrow's labour, hard time you might,
You *do* swallow everything, make null plenty;
But I forbid your wasting years one terrible crime,
Do not etch your lines on my love's face, empty
The world if and as you must, but leave him, time.
Should you sweep him away by a hair's breadth, as you will,
Still my love will his clement youth on this timeless page fulfil.

20

Your face - fine nose, fresh skin, the engraving eye -
Surpasses all feminine beauty's extravagant paint.
You are nature's marvel, prodigious producer of sighs
From admirers and adversaries distant and near, nor faint
Your gaze that's true and reads as much as read;
You plunder men's looks, ravage women's souls,
Beauty is your armor, yet not war but love instead
Is your mettle, you are born to license women to be whole
Even though you pass by me who knows you better
Than any woman can, with them you master pleasure
As you master your will that pricks life into matter
Like a god, none can bridle you nor attain the measure
Of love you have retained for me upon which to draw,
So you might pleasure your adoring lovers all the more.

21

I will not hearsay make with my listing verse
To paint beauty with elaborate heavens,
Flowers that burst with radiance, I won't rehearse
The sun and the moon, the stars that are leavened
With nothing better than the mechanics of sound.
I am not about to circumnavigate nature's signs,
To brocade a seeming paradise by words bound.
No, I would that art foretell truly, my lines
Be cast from my heart to draw you my love
Before me as august, dear as any babe in arms,
But not quite as wildly innocent; I shall remove
All impediment of graceful lies, customed charms
That are more gold than gold, then to be sincere
I shall compose an ode that's bold, true and clear.

The mirror cannot my reflecting age belie
When you, still young and beautiful, bind me.
But when time steals to live in your face, rust your eye,
Then shall death, time's server, come to find me.
Your beauty is my all that skins my entered heart
And makes me silver, the mirror does not blind me.
How then can age on me descend, evening start
When your day is young enough to pretend? Be wary
With expense of yourself as I slow the years
Not for me but for you in youth made merry
By engagement to my eye, no insolent tears
Shall reside there, none, their salt eat not my skin.
I am an emblem, proud and right, fluttering in the wind
For your beauty day and night, let it die and you have sinned.

So undisclosed am I to my reformed self
I'm like an actor broken from his speech,
I stutter and dissolve or like a frenzied wolf
Distempered with rage, I cannot reach
That level of trust that sports of discretion
Which would teach me to lodge art in love's rite.
So falter I in loving as I should, make concession
To endorse my own extreme love's might.
Where once voice spoke, lips can only mutter,
Let my writing part make up by its dumb show
The migrations of a longing heart that shutters
A secret language only lovers can truly know.
I despair of my drunken words that faint and reel,
So hear with eyes love's print as fine and pure as steel.

My eye touches you with its painter's art,
Before my gaze you become, in it you purely are
Beauty's form as outlined in the fable of my heart.
Your colours lend flint to my fire, your shining is my star.
To prime the canvas of my body's frame
You must look through to my divining skill
To speculate on the ore of your beauty's claim
On my forming eye where my heart does will.
Then you'll see what eye for eye has done,
My eyes have spun your shape, and yours
For me have lifted my heart like the rising sun
That lights all to wait upon you and open doors
For beauty's theatre to enter through, make day from night,
Yet my eyes your beauty see, but wanting are your heart's delight.

My stars are not instruments but suns
That prick the dark when day's put out.
I have missed fame, no public honour runs
Into my name, I am pressed for favours to scout
A triumph or two that may identify me, but joy
Which comes unannounced I honour most.
Those who fawn and make themselves toys
For great men's favours are like flowers
Which open and close on whims that coast
The moods of superior lights, those rising towers
Of influence that flank them; their praise, their boasts
Like the world, are husks that weigh a ton.
I would rather love and be loved by one
Than play the world's fiddle that ends before it's begun.

You whose very presence is my air,
Who duty teaches my heart and submitted eye,
To you I send this envoy with a lover's care
That seeks unplucked truth, yet doing duty my
Wit is sullen and bare, wanting words to speak
And pen as duty should; yet I'll sign my submission
And hope your soul shall receive and seek
From my unwitting duty my wit's admission
And make you intelligence of me who pays you
A duty more favoured by my native star;
Thus duty whispered shall with words fair and true
Find honey not for what you do but who you are,
So may I wax my stuttering wit where
I may my duty make yours to share.

How sweet is slumber in the billows of a bed,
How dreams are welcome to exhausted arms and legs
And spirit, occult rivers that run through my head;
But sleep is not cultivated, left with its dregs
I enter a pilgrimage to you who tunnel me
With a darkness only a blind man can devise,
So does my yearning heart its chemistry revise
In the cells of my brain, a symmetry that channels me
To my soul's imaginary sight that enters from the skin
Of my closed eyes which dark concede next to insanity.
By day I labour and scheme for mundane humanity
By night I am chained to dreams, I neither win
Nor lose my fate but siphon energy and wait
To grow a heart for yours before it's too late.

Neither by day nor by night let me forget
How empty I am, how absence from you numbs
Me to day's returning light, I am nailed to regret
When night's narrow hours cross me with crumbs
Of your form that feeds a mind drawn out in moods
That night's journey construes; I am still
Where in the ocean dark your memory occludes
But not in a peace I own, and sullen day will
Bring me torture too rounded for me instead;
I sell my sleep to night to banquet on your face,
Convening night's dark with psalms for the dead
Who at least are absence's absence without place
Or promise of presence as day is drained into dread night,
Yet I'd still be yours even when I pass finally from light.

When I feel discarded like worn-out laces
When I am inclined to moan my public fate,
To look with envy on the deeds, the market traces
Of others seeming better than I in wealth and estate,
Rich with art and laughing company day and night
That make my own felt pleasures insipid things,
I breed in me a double-discontent, disclosing flight
From true success and self that loving you brings
When I am a private sun illuminate with inner life,
A rising song that frees itself from fret of earth,
Espouses your love's mirror that surpasses strife.
When I think of you I am light twinkling with birth
Of absolving joy, as your love restores myself to me
So my heart discards becoming for what I am about to be.

When I am drawn to screen the past
I am siphoned by loss of those I loved, cast
Now in inter-stellar dark where time wrests
All instruments of identity. I am struck by the press
Of memory which crosses cares and tells of grief;
The loss of so many beloved sights which dressed
The ardour of my granted presence the brief
Of flattering moment's infinity at the time.
These rendered scenes are choked with salt of my eyes
Which makes the outward glass of me dark with grime
That cakes wintered conscience; I see the ties
That had made me, dissolve, passage only is real;
But when I think of you in heart and mind,
You make resort of me, my loss is left behind.

The excess of your being contains all those I loved,
Buried by their recession in the eye of my heart
That lacks their once dear abiding obsession; I am moved
To retire their absence now gravely lost, their formal part
Washed away by the intimate art of tears shed as their due
From my interested eyes that buried their account in grief.
Thus I was guided from the station of the old to the new.
In you these extinguished lamps are fired, brief
Removed lights that chasten me with returning loss
Which victories were, pricked with youth whose cry
Was insolent pleasure not bowed sorrow, that cross
Which makes images of lovers tomorrow in the heart of the eye.
They have passed through these shifting forms their sum of parts
And mine left entire in your substance whose eye enfolds my heart.

32

When you survive me as you will, and God,
When death makes darling dust of me as cover,
So a separate veil is drawn and I am unshod,
And you by chance once more discover
This written part of me that day and night
Forgot and took you with them for a time,
Compare this restoration to you with the random lights
That preserve the day you receive; for their rhymes
Are seductive resort for those who live lightly in mind
And heart, so forgetful, mark their life - this art of mine
Is made for you who shall in me succeed to find
A life more equal perhaps in love than a poet's shine.
Yet remember me not for styles that wing from me your loss
But for the love I bear you which substance is, more than gloss.

I may not read the sun's fluid pace with impartial eye,
First it graces the highest peak with its liquid gold
Then pastures green it implements with heavenly light, fly
Night and all dark and sullen things that night enfolds.
But stray winds gather earth's yielding damp to clouds that race
Covering sun, light and gold, that basely rack the sky's open face
With surly transit across our eyes sacked and found empty-dull
With sudden theft of precious morning dew; now space
Is condemned to choking shadows, to air that's full
Of soured change that shifts our moods; even so my sun did shine
One morning finding me first in place to receive its candour,
His imperious light like the early sun was but shortly mine
Before its rising was put out, all spent its splendour.
Yet my love holds fast, to him I shall my best part render.

It hurts me so to receive you and let you go
When you present an inclement face to me.
Why do you promise not with pretty words so
Much as with expressions more silently
Spoken by face and eye, epithets of your body
That make me travel from the capture
Of my mentality to wear with you the shoddy
Day you break with me, I am without rapture
Then and no man can find the physic to cure
What is in the face and heart of me, you may
Repent and pander your shame, let open the shore
Of your flooding eyes, these natural satisfactions say
The prayers of your sorrow but they are weak relief
Even so, your ambient tears are rain on my belief.

Your faults are set to the discord in nature's tone,
No more are they than mud that crystal fountains bear,
Nor faded moon made muddy with cloud that atones
For its sensual waking play in lovers' eyes when they share
The secret fragments of the hearts which break
Where they most fail to see; all have blind faults
Even I in this small space dressed with words that stake
Our good faith with vain temerity; we cannot call halt
To our excesses without a price that us will devoid,
So I against myself will remain miscreant, in war
With right and wrong that flow in my blood deployed
To all my central parts; I am here to accede to acts
That to my faulty sight make rash accessory of you,
I cite you then in my plea that you may find me guilty too.

To belong is not to lose the self that seeks
To belong to make one of two yet remains.
So shall my appetite retain the sins that reek
Only of me not you, we are two that stain
Each other with our one undivided love
Thrown together so we, two in one, might marry
Our senses to our minds and coo like turtle doves.
Though we are mined by sole defects that carry
Charges against you and me which deplete hours
From our store of delight, our double faces turn
Away as we suit each other's intent and cower
Behind encircling guilt and shame that burns
Us into delinquency; yet I love you by design,
In spite of twin separation, I am yours and you are mine.

37

To look upon and be in attendance on your youth,
Its sinewed beauty, wit and gracious deeds
Is happy compromise to my dusty parts, with truth
Made fecund and tumultuous free, so am I freed
From my barren season's downward path by receipt
Of your tempting rise to tease time with your qualities royal
That crown the several prancing contrasts which make conceit
With your youth's blatant entitlement, for I am entrusted, loyal
Slave to the substantial accidents of your sovereign prime
Who in their unwitting abundance restore my stock,
And by your parts am I remedied, repeated like rhyme
By your concocted beauty and wit, I am opened by your lock.
Whatever is best in a world spun and refined, I wish for you,
My simple wish is burning hot, it is a fire that runs me through.

I cannot create without the grain of your beauty,
No invention can bear to stain with grafted mark,
Depend on prose that ensures your absence; my duty
Is to book you, to submit and learn to pen the stark
Truth of this purchase against the grain of my verse.
I paint with words from the light of your eyes,
For words are blight without their shine, my voice terse
When your substance is scarce, meaning shaded with lies
That play the devil's role in me; you are ten-time muse I call
Upon to rehearse my solvent art and make it flesh
For my muse's part, so I may sing and trawl
My inner worth and be married to words made fresh
By love for you removed from common parlance, then raise
My art to double me in doubling you, poised with artful praise.

I cannot praise you when you and I are one
I cannot with candied words sugar my better part
Which you incarnate play and shine like the sun.
How can my praise flatter my own heart
Unless for praise's sake we rebut our desire
To be one, return to our own place and name
Which distance give, needed space to require
The world to see the undiluted you, the flame
That lights my eyes; this banishment of self, discard
From self in self, single the whole design,
Makes sour passing time retract from its hard
Deception with scenes of love that ground my mind.
Thus my compulsion for praise of you makes division an art
By dividing one from one so that my enabled praise may start.

40

You caper my love and still want for more
But the love you've garnished is my source
All that I have to give from my entire store.
Open then the palm of your heart, your mind's force
Bring to bear on my emergency for you to care;
My love's loves are all yours to have as your silk,
Can I be blamed if after you I have no more to share?
You receive my substance as a cat receives milk
From the keeper he deigns to own, you may steal,
Eccentric thief, love's image from my eyes that burned
Out of love for you, make me blind to conceal
My dearth when ill-used my love is not returned.
You pat me with your paws, with my grieving love play for dead,
For this injury I'll not wait on you with hate but love you more instead.

Your youth and your vigour congruent fit
Thus take liberty as their right when I am sent
Out of your mind and your heart when you hit
Upon her who is beauty's prey, a willing victim sent
By the gods to tempt you, so easily won away
From me; you are temptation's monument, you woo
To win another fragile heart, but I am here to stay
Your wondering with words you do not hear, cue
For my chiding that bears your beauty from my seat.
Yet you are beauty and deceit, a gainsaying youth,
Your blood's a sun of its own, your light meets
Who it wills and when and where, breathing false truths
Without a care; you pluck me from my heart, share
That which only belongs to you as carelessly as air.

I see you and him discourse head
And heart in happy colloquy, I wonder
At you and he so attentive a pair fed
On instant adoration, I'm not cruel to tear asunder
What providence has wrought to love and to hold.
But that you belong not to me is my fertile grief.
Yet my pain is soft-hearted neither detached nor cold
To your attachment that so closely enfolds a thief
It cannot prise apart to let light between your souls.
You love him as yourself who does bridle me
As you engage and I lose your gazing eyes
To your new lover's state, I contemplate and see
A new rising sun from the love you draw, the ties
You break and take as one, as you love him for me.

My loving pricks out your shadow's shadow from the night
When my lids deploy their cloth, the light that day shows
To minded eyes who would rather see you with inward sight
Through the telescope of dreams whose stories throw
You in relief when with lively ardour I declare good sleep
To be my ally in the crusade for you whose shadow plans
Such harmonious survey across my heart with supple and deep
Attainment where none is, before your beauty's birth scans
And makes me stark, vain with your delighting shape.
But to see you in the malted light of my descending day
Is more glorious than the morning sun to one who cannot escape
The tutelage of your native blessing's script, I may
By this daily light learn to essay myself through love of you,
Make night day, day night, and with these images, to love be true.

If my thought was my body, heavy and opaque,
Not the spirit which is quick with love and light,
Ariel's cousin curving in flight from earth's weight,
I would not lack you when you're absent, despite
The dancing figures of my mind that fly land and sea.
But from my empty place I am and can only be husk,
My restless thought has left me fanatical with you to be.
You a million distances away, too arduous a task
For this ephemeral flesh of mine given to grief for lack
Of you now your substance is removed, I sound
My leisure enforced by loss with inward sighs black
As jet, I am made petty by the chains of thought bound
To you by the fantastical distance that makes you free,
I am nought, without you I am rendered apart from me.

Two parts of my four, feathered air, feeding fire,
Those high-bounded elements with you reside.
My thought has withdrawn and also my desire
To your court to make petition so you may decide
For me with tender clemency; when these two are gone
I am halved and sink into the mud and slime
Of melancholy seeming without reprieve, until I'm borne
Back to my entire complement returning to my prime,
These two ambassadors resolve me with happy news
Of your health and disposition, I'm assured for a while
You are in good state, your eye is mine, your views
Make sequence to those beliefs that hold me for trial.
But when I am filled without you again, my joy departs,
So too my measured eyes for you, I am left where I start.

46

My eye and warring heart are at civil strife
On which or which may master your sight.
My eye your surface does bring to life
Sufficient to its own, my heart makes light
Your beauty more deeply your spirit to bare
Thus move with it beyond the eye's ambition
To a cloistered, holy place outside eye's care.
Heart to heart may fit with heartfelt decision
But the eye with heart's appearance is never satisfied
Which claims a surer part of you than senses know,
A surface truth where eye to eye is nearly implied.
So the battle from heart to eye and eye to heart flows
Without giving way, until a truce is declared,
Eye retains its part, heart its own and you are shared.

47

My heart and eye a fertile compact make
To declare alliance between thought and look.
When my eye is bereft of your gaze it takes
A leaf from my heart's accounting book
And reads the balance sheet of my love.
Another time the eye to you the heart leads
Implanted with images pupilled inwardly above
Meretricious change that time concedes.
Thus when you are not in time with me
Your picture and my love combine to stay
In heart and eye, your absence is therefore free
To roam since in my eye and heart your legend plays.
Or if, for a moment, I make dalliance in thought or sight,
Your picture restores their erring to their senses with its delight.

48

I bind and lock all slavish precious cares
In secret hiding places for my exclusive use
Not to be plucked by others' blatant stares
And consummation, these pleasures abstruse
Are, as they are dear to me but not dearest
As are you who come and go as you please, free
As the wind that restrains stubborn heat with clearest
Cool of touch; my comfort, my grief as you are to be
Agent for your own distraction, prey to eyes that just
Snare you thus, so your embodied love from me to bar;
You graze where you will in the meadow of my breast
Then turn away for greener pastures, distant, fresh, far
From my solicitude, even thus your rapture so dear
Is too slightly honest to resist felony of the theft I fear.

49

Against that potential time when absent good
Shall make potent absence's presence felt,
When your eye that was warm flesh turns to wood,
Dull clouds your visage draw, when I am dealt
With frowns from you instead of smiles,
When love's vintage turns to vinegar, sour
With sullen reasons to avert you with the guile
That makes a scarecrow of me, predicating power
Is yours, mine is only to love you, so I make strong
My cause to live by knowing the desert in my heart;
My hand shall rear itself in oath to geld the wrong
You shall commit me with argued causes that impart
In sultry depositions your denials of my wounded claim,
For I love with heart which is to love more than in name.

Each heavy step, each slow mourned for second
Away from you to an end I do not know nor care,
Says this to me as I am slowly beckoned
From you whose journey I do not share,
With passing time you are made into stone
No spur can prick to life nor bring to mind
As I am made from you; I am torn in half, bone
Of husk that rolls on, the better part left behind
To couple with your ghostly self starved
Into unreliable memory, we have no choice,
Moving on, riding heavy waves of time, carved
From your absence that reads me with moist
Tears and sighs as I am pricked on by blame
Parting from you, my grief cannot be tamed.

To travel from you with steps slow
And sluggish, I am at least content
For I would move as a tree than go
At a gallop from you my sole extent.
I take no light to make slow theft of speed,
This sorry departure; but to return, restore
My horse's pace, swift as thought is my steed.
This beast shall race angels, even light score
To reach its goal with burning haste to post
Your presence with you again, my horse
Flying, I am tributary of your grace, host
To all I desire, expanding as I run the course,
To divide its width from you I am not slow
You are my music, you make my blood flow.

52

To make timely pleasure is to learn
Pleasure's timed, particular, salted ecstasies, few
Fewer still made more precise to discern
With mind and heart and accrued senses new
With unusual use, so I am richly thirsted, this rationed
Beauty of yours chastens my act locked in desire
That would feast on you like a panther fashioned
By black night with avid eyes on fire,
Jewels buried in fur chased with gold
That veils the dream which you encloses
With a blush of lauds, his rare pride you fold
Yourself around with your current; but he disposes
The pluck of impatience, fastens the senses, his will
Aligned, so that he may rely in your treasure still.

As blessed rain does parched earth revive,
So your beauty restores my wooden gaze to life.
Your substance which so brightly is derived
That all about it is mere form, shadowy midwife
To your one real birth in a world grown counterfeit;
In your sight all myth and heroes can survive
Only as antidotes, poor preludes to you who create
Simply by living in your spring, your sun gives
Me heat who knows you for what you are, no mask
Can iterate you without blasphemy; with you I live,
Without you I become a model of shadows, to ask
This play to be otherwise performed is a vain task,
To see you in pretended images that have no heart,
Like you, your grace to all rich blessings imparts.

54

Beauty is more than eye does or eye can see,
More beauty leases the more its essence distilled
From an inward honesty which like a sun frees
Beauty to be itself as a rose that's filled
With perfume which sweetly colours the air;
Yet wild roses dance as wildly in the breeze,
Wear the same thorns, their colour as fair,
But show they only virtue's slant by unsung degrees
And so entrance the distracted eye on a summer noon;
When they die none do requiem as their natural due,
Their fragile passage from life forgotten as soon
As day is down; but to their housed, individual cousin who
Honoured is in print when scything dark invades its bed sorrow
To endow, so you my beloved, shall be honoured on the morrow.

55

None of the pavilions nor arching domes
Made for splendid public pomp and state
Shall outlive these words of mine which from
Your beauty flow to live on this page and wait
For readers posterity to find whose hearts are ripe
To contemplate; statues are raised and destroyed
By revolution and war, too blatant, they are wiped
Away by history's gales or simply forgotten, deployed
On their blighted pedestals to cramped corners; burnt
By fire or cracked by degenerate time you shall not be,
By this you will record against death's seal, return
To your magnetic youth whenever read, you shall see
Yourself through eyes that the future bestows, and signs
You with this refining verse, lest ears be deaf and eyes be blind.

Desire may be a force for an hour or two
But force it and it is dead, decimated, blunted
Through use, appetite may remain through
Imagination's drawing habit to be shunted
From image to image like a gambler's dice
That rolls for a double, so bank up your desire
Let not dull satisfaction erode your will, suffice
The day to wrest tomorrow as your act restores new fire
To your winking eye, for this love sliding Eros pays
To enlighten with playful artifice, this fair return
Of interest shall your capital accrue, new ways
To spend your energy with me, new ways to burn,
To receive and grant love, which being used, knows
Your summer to invest you with potency to bestow.

57

You make good currency of me to spend
As you will and when but I do not complain,
My dependent time is mercury, it has no end
In view save what you pin on it and do; slain
By love I am your slave who makes time for you.
When you are away from me the hours rust my being
But no bitter distrust gathers there when you say adieu;
I patch the black of nights alone by innocent seeing
In my serving eye how seeming good you distant are,
Not asking how good you may be in your affairs
Abroad, how others are near when I am far,
I am your servant who is your pleasure to wear;
So love is broken in, that you obedience in me instill
Who serves and loves your expense for good or ill.

I am that slave of yours that makes all acts submission,
I do not think of curbing even your sighs, never mind
The measure you withdraw from me, I am not in manumission
From service to you though the hours you take away blind
The time I yield to you with other service that with leisure
You buy on the wealth of your smile and will.
Bent to suffer for loss of you, my pain is at your pleasure,
I am nature's patience, no thought of injury, the drill
Of your deeds that make impotence of me, tame me
As is their due, I am your list you carry on charter,
You bear me in your hold, it is for you to blame me
Without cause as I am branded by you who may barter
Me for any distraction that comes your way,
I wait only as passive night for your rising day.

Were I to bend to something new with time's run
When time went round rather than straight ahead,
My aim would be loosened before time had begun.
If I were to see you in some ancient book, the dead
Image of your face, I would wonder at the fault
That time's round could suffer on seeing you again.
Your time is run but it shall run anew, time to see
Me reading you in characters past and future plain
To the prophetic eye that picks out the pedant stars' decrees.
I know not whether we are today good judges
Of men and their deeds, or yesterday's round made
Bad good as we claim not to do bearing grudges
Against time's way with us, but with time we fade
As we fall victim to replacing years that us invade.

Jostling seconds mount the rising day, step
Into descending night, their rearing crowd
Devise your form which from nothing leapt
Into sight, in summary light and dark by proud
Degrees you grew into healthy maturity alight
With youth and beauty, but relentless run
The seconds their marathon time, by their flight
Draw parallels on your brow, as the silent sun
Your setting too is fixed your waxing to confound,
For nothing stays the pace of time that nothing ends,
From nothing starts your handsome face, crown
Of your presence before my eye which by this sends
A message to nothing's eternity, to the *now* of your face
Fixing worth with new lines for you in this flimsy space.

Am I kept awake by your spirit's watch
When I am alone, gelid with your lack?
Is it your absent eye that would match
Mine for tears which ready flow, protract
The alchemy of loss from you? I am
Too much with you when you leave, alone
I brood the intimacy I've lost which like a dam
Holds the power of my desire that's thrown
Off balance by sleepless night; am I under scrutiny
For you to search for ripe jealousy's sake?
No, this love we share is ample but not due to me
So that you can travel yet from my spring and break
Surface from the bread of my soul, you in me are guarded
By my own love which by yours is coldly disregarded.

Love of self closer than the cover of skin
That restrains my soul, shades me from my heart;
Self-love's conceit, self-love without self-love within
For the branded sin which burns in my every part,
No remedy I find being grounded by my own regard
Which self-love factors even in the words that bare me,
I wallow in warm waters of deceit, modesty discarded,
I am bound by my love so trophied none can share me
Above all other clay, more worthy grace than any face
None dares to match my seeming pedigree refined;
But when I look in the mirror, in that reflecting space
I see the surface that I am, antiquity's haven, defined
By speaking lines which ruse the love and pain
I have for you whose beauty washes my own love's stain.

See how young he is, imagine how he will be
When years have cast their seasons
Angling in their round, his face shall still be
His but not mine today, dull reason
Makes object of time explaining all away,
A history of causes summoned to be read
By dry eyes that study dust but do not stay
Their knowingness to see in youth age fed
With lines and memories and slowing blood;
Look at him and love, prepare for his grave
So distant now but nearer than rose to mud.
For such sombre rapture some love I save
To greet him when we're old, he shall not be seen
As do these words which print him as he has been.

No doubt that time unwinds what's been
To reduce smooth beauty to lines of dust,
But when the heart must see what's seen
Between youth and age a shifting crust
That moves to quake our selves and raze
The gorgeous palaces of the world, move earth
To water and water to sullen earth, each phase
A seven point rise and decline; I feel the dearth
Of passion that shall come to stop you and me,
This winging prophecy will cover the sun in black.
It teaches me the philosophy of decay when sea
And land do each other confound back to back.
This thought is a dying one that makes me weep
To know that this fair youth I love I shall not keep.

Nothing is immortal this side of the moon
Nothing beyond, nor radium nor sea,
Nothing escapes the exactitude of time, no boon
Is provided for you and me to hold, to free
From decay, the rust of age outlives itself;
How can fragile beauty that eyes the living breath,
How can harmonies that bell the ear with wealth,
Like the salmon out-leap sturdy death?
This alien winter lowers the blood, shrinks
The sun into its mortal eye. I am dark
With thoughts that age me to the brink,
I am an abyss which all things mark
With prior desolation; where can I hide
From this awe your beauty here supplied?

66

I do not complain I simply state:
I am weary, worn to the gum with masks
That pretend qualities that do not relate
To what is simple and true, we create tasks
That feed credulity, feebly dissipate good deeds
And straight honesty which is never tried
Despite the eulogies of worthy men who put greed
Aside for themselves to grow fat on; despised
Is honour, for what is it? And virtue is declined
By clever doctors of lies, the law applied is theirs
To make and break as they will, by these inclined
To skills a conjurer would vie for, no honest man care;
No more this soil to bind me, I would better die -
But this beginning would rob me of your loving eye.

He imprisons beauty and grace
Brings impiety to the fore,
Infected with insolence his face
Launches a scarab eye dead to the core.
Why should beauty be sentenced to spin,
Grace lose its head, all joy suspend?
If not the devil then he is the twin
Who paints shadows that youth pretends,
His blood is thirsty and rusts within,
He is a charlatan dry and uncouth, bends
Poor nature beggared and broken to sin,
She is made unnatural by his bitter spend.
Yet I am sworn to nature to her defend
That you might love's nature comprehend.

Training night with his visage, he rakes
Dreams to expound with abysses, falling
Away from what once was, he wakes
To a past before his cheeks laid appalling
Tenure on time's passing, before his head
Was moved from beauty that opened the tap
Of life, epitome of youth's explosion read
And lived at high season, now his face a map,
An etching that reveals the living marrow
Of truth without notes to betray a grace unseen,
He confers with his peers in doubled sorrow
Trying false summers with their wintered green.
From him astounded nature does surely draw
What false art cannot form from beauty's store.

Your outward form is so firmly fair
That you with other's eyes complete
Your beauty's margin disposed to care
For show, but with the secret inner seat
Of your soul you must show its light
So tongues may speak, minds compare
The outward with the tender inward sight
That looks to curve your mind where
All living declines into its several parts
For you to bestow with envy what we see.
Is it to read revelation with lips from heart
That scripture shows your deeds? You may be
More than simple beauty, for this dream grows
To an entire love, both good and bad to know.

70

Your beauty and spirit are filters for lies
That grow in abundance about you who fare
The better when slanders your worth despise;
Your fair acts then rise up like fish to bear
Your hallmark libel fibres with every word
Spoken of you, and by you checked, so prove
Libel's suit that with eager ears is duly heard
By those who train libel to be not easy to disprove,
Thus acclaim you rich with whispered vice.
But I know you have shed your younger days
Without more than a bruise or two, wisdom's price
To dye you into your naked heartfelt ways.
I will not sit in parliament with this hunting crush
That with crowded defamations makes you blush.

Dream not me into life again when I'm dead,
Do not contemplate the joys you had with me.
When I have gone from this world, when it's said
The bells toll for me alone, when God's decree
Is writ for my return into earth, and dust with dust
Shall marry to print my presents no more
Than this verse, do not recall (or pay you must)
The heart that wrote it; for I love you with sure
Economy so that you can live and found your love
With living without rehearsing my septic name,
Even with sad voice and tearful eyes look above
Your grief for I am no longer signed the same
As when you held my hand and searched my face,
You alone distil with passing words my empty space.

For should the world ask you to praise
What virtue I may have that is not said,
That should your solvent words raise,
Do not say so, for I am not but dead
And my name which was sweet on tongue,
My face the eye's adornment, are fled
From you and lie buried, they belong
No more to you to endow with quality true
Or false, certainly more than posthumous I
Can ever grace no matter how long through
The trial I submit and shade to when I die.
So sing not of me or my history's soil, defy
The temptation that makes the plaintive lyre cry
To consecrate your grief, all speech of me deny.

Now winter grows me into season
Insight flows into the heart with ice.
As trees grow bare, youth's treason
Leaves me for another spring with nice
Inches not noticed; an ache here and there,
A momentary loss, but gathering pace as do
Waves reaching the shore, I am where
All men must to account be and endure through
Fading light the shadows that come to play
In me, you see in the ash glints of the fire
Of youth excelled, which night shall take away,
Then on my bed I shall be disclosed, expire,
Quench my eyes for the light of another day,
Shortly before its end, this life with love you stay.

Rest content even when for a time grief
Borrows you, for what is dead disguises
Form that eternal inner holds in relief,
But when dissolved, the cool spirit rises
Without the body's grasp, from these lines
That you shall recite with melting heart
That touch upon with sight of varied signs
Of me which trace me in you as I depart
From eloping day for coming night; yours
Is my soul that on my form's decease your breath
And voice shall shine my gold, with vision restore
The springing sense that hides me from death,
So you have and will have when I die
My spirit if yourself to these words apply.

My dreaming is fed by you, kept alive
By what you are and might ascribe being
Both true and untrue, your image I strive
To keep within the curtilage of my mind seeing
Through my reaching eye which you desires
To maintain in full panoply with your star.
Now I am rich with you, now a miser who acquires
Only the dust you leave behind, now near now far
When the world at large takes hold of you, trains
Its whispers to describe and engulf, when out
Of your governing sight I'm made insane
By lack of you, then I'm a land in drought.
Thus do I yearn and glut on you each day
Either with which I live, or without I fade away.

Why are my words so battle-scarred?
Why do they always read the same?
Why do my seasons repeat, so new is barred?
Iteration runs in grooves so to claim
A compound herd that bans new speech
Unperturbed before it's born, only the old stores
What I want to say, and what you teach;
Your sun matures my verse, its vintage deplores
Raw untried ways to rhyme you, my sole affair.
So my sounds are derived and origin will not part,
Speaking new what's already said, I do not care
To say more nor cannot, you're my *a la carte*.
As day and night come and go
So my love repeats its private show.

Restless time unsettles your ways,
In the mirror your searching eyes find
Small changes, the coming print that betrays
Your slight purchase on present self behind
Which lies time's libel set to swallow you.
Your skin which from silk to parchment shows
Your slowing senses their extent and through
Their growing limits memory itself knows
Nothing richer than what was youth's impertinence;
As you travel from your centre, so you print
Your children midwived from your lips' governance,
Made speech to press and from you take on another tint.
So these progeny released on the page
Shall your conception's dying assuage.

Can muses exist when you are here?
How strong your influence has on my verse,
Your eyes are the beauty my words do bear,
The world to recreate, new words disburse
When you and I are gone several centuries hence.
Thus you shall always become what you already are,
Adding to your beauty future beauty's recompense.
You teach rough manners to refine, thus to bar
Crude design when they contemplate what I compile;
Be proud of my resolve to speak of you and write
So others' work may be born in authentic style
Where act and art do grace refine for every sight.
Your mortal tone makes immortal my singing art
With heaven's grace it stays as you and I depart.

Your capital lies in your face and form
You my verse storm with the pleasure
You grant my eye, my seeking words born
Of love of you, want to save your treasure
With my discourse that marks you right.
But my speech is paltry with epithets few
Understand save those who know your light.
Those who spoke and wrote you well, knew
That painting with sugared virtues your face
Was for simple robbers who would go to hell.
All praises which of you print has no trace
Than that you print yourself, your cheeks tell
Another tale truer still who none can say
Better than you to whom love only knows the way.

Words are short with me when of you I write,
I know I'm surpassed by another who better speaks
Of you than I can sue, and indeed this writer invites
You to a perfection I cannot adorn, oblique
With modesty I lack extremities you to explain;
You are interstellar space and ocean-deep,
So he may float upon the craft of his gain
On me who make from my poverty's steep
Descent measured lines for you to enjoy.
I would be a minnow at least to his shark
At play, mendicant I may be, but I employ
Heart and mind that suit closer you to mark.
Even if he win you with clever words, still
I know my love for you shall prevail your will.

Death claims all that we know in mind
If not in heart, time passing these words shall stake
New minds, new hearts, whether hart or hind,
When you and I shall to earth ourselves take,
But my words will astound themselves and fly
To eyes and ears yet to come, and epitaph make
Of you from their flight, then I alone shall die
Passing you on to modern souls who shall long
For your beauty to savour in their mind's eye.
There is no complaint then if I do not belong
To those who with the lime of praise apply
Subversion in their hearts, my verse's strong
Charge your youth and energy shall pen
So you shall live and love more dearly then.

82

Send for them who would of you speak
With rich gaudy colours making vain
What lives clear by its own, should you seek
More flattery than the truth that reigns
Over my tongue, you're not sealed to my muse,
You can wander where you will to refine
New precipitations of youth that they may fuse
Time to a stop; you're as wise as you are kind,
Your wisdom surpasses my stamp as is your right.
But those who would devise such overlaid words
To you declaimed have no hearing, have no sight
For that calm innocence that in silence is heard.
And their queasy verse has no better claim
But paltry stuff that only seconds your fame.

You need no words no fading colours!
You are your own art and drawing quill.
To paint you is to fail, invite pale dolour
Displace your living midsummer will.
You are more endowed in word and deed
Than any foreign skill can surely depict.
Your flower too rich, too potent your seed
To be numbered by art alone that inflicts
The artist obtuse with dreams which depart
From true sense of you, so silent shall I remain,
So silent your beauty shall stay rooted to your part
Nor your sovereign form be laid to others' acclaim.
For I know your eyes more life create and expand
Than the poverty of my clumsy lips or mumbling hand.

Words merely salvage you who are more
In accord with unprismatic light all one
That shows you as you, who is entirely sure
Of your spectrum, the eye's alembic sun
Without equal, no pen can truly praise.
If he that would write you as God creates new
Perfection of yourself no one can keep nor raise
Another like from you, then he shall true
Ground make with his enhanced story.
Let him draw you out like a ray of light
Not sullying your nature nor dull your glory,
Then shall he blind all others from your sight.
Such a picture would receive God's curse
Unless its praises only your form rehearse.

85

My muse is discreet in demeanour, triste and still,
While others praise with garnished words, their
Phrases complicate your simple beauty's will.
They hone their pen, subtract honey from the air,
Write with grace notes here and there you to laud,
And I, amazed by their cries, raise my eyes and say
"Amen", "It's right", with hand on heart I you applaud.
So I smile and say with my watching mind, and obey
My sovereign retreating muse who with silent deeds
Defines my love for you leaving rising words behind,
My flame is doubled in me for love of you that feeds
With my muteness with which I see their praises blind.
They think they describe with gelded breath your face,
And so with candied arbitrage they would me displace.

I am sorely tempted to say his felon verse
Took mine and strangled at birth to lull
My thoughts that turbulent dreams rehearse
Of you immured in the concert of my skull.
Was it his brilliant words that carry light
Rebelling against staid complement of virtue
That tainted me? No, not his words nor might
Of Lucifer deny me my course to skirt you
With the proper passion that bides in me
To print another smiling version of your face;
I am too impervious to him to fear, and flee
My wit, I wait the words that fill this place,
But when he captures not your soul but your form,
My lines are shy to show themselves - the curtain's drawn.

Such votaries as my paucity may pant out
For you whose dearness no price can keep,
Are siblings to the nothing that's air; I doubt
I can match your parings where I am too deep
In the mediocrity of flesh, my ties to you
Are shallow and shall doubtless die when away
You turn your eye from the collar of my love through
Which I claim to know you; I am what I betray,
A levy on your riches you now grant me freely
Knowing not my worth nor yet your own.
So your bounty shall run its course then I'll dearly
Pay when your sense makes you solvent and I'm thrown.
Thus with the flattery of sleep I dream I'm your hunter and prey
But on waking I become a notary of loss with the coming day.

When you decide to turn on me and deride
I shall your double be and speak me out
To champion my wrong; I shall be at your side.
Stamp the virtue of your biting words, flout
My demeanour's lost pride, knowing better my faults
Than you, I shall better accost your own to arrest
Their salty acts for which I am practised, halt
All summary convictions saved for me who attest
Your echoing honesty that reckons me what I am.
So you shall gain as I lose and gain again twice
To bend to your story that upends me as a sham,
The injuries I claim shall submit to a double vice.
Thus my love is proof by you made strong
Yet the honour you pay me proves it wrong.

89

You can report on me my several faults
Edit offence and I shall add severe gloss
To the wrong you prepare for me, halt
All goodness that betrays me to cross
Your subtle reasons which complain defection.
Call up my lameness and I shall limp in mind
To your dismissal of my health, imperfection
Only by sight of you that in me sadly finds.
I shall not present myself before your dock
To repeat what you now prevent, nor dwell
On the vintage of your name that was my rock,
Lest my former addiction should you more repel.
So I repeal myself, make way so you may go,
Free yourself, so I my absence may bestow.

If you are to leave me, my sorry love discard,
Then wind the sheet, deplete yourself before
The world extends to nail me, to bring me hard
News of my disgrace earned and banked I'm sure
But never so bitter as your loss, do not drop
Your guard let out the carrion flight that picks
My dross as afterthought to raise pain's crop
Ready for reaping in the act to come, stick
To *now* before the common stock of public woes
Rise up to extract their teeming, stiffening spite,
The rigour of my esteem, your whip show
And your bite, take my vigour, that part right
Next to my heart, then shall I stronger be to stand
All other scorn delivered me by fortune's hand.

What interest have I in riches and potent skill,
What in position that others aspire, what strength
Can accentuate me, what intellect or will?
Some souls crave these and go to every length
To capitalise in and proudly coxcomb the day
Which every pleasure slides dancing to deceive
Yet still remove them to earthly joy and sensual play.
But I am not one to foster these and with thirst receive
Their posturing accord on my flesh and person, I have one -
You who better these passing revelries with smiling love
That wounds me into my desired need, so I shun
All captioned copies that mimic your seed, this dove
Which flies me higher to heaven than all else here,
But your neglect is one treachery, one loss I fear.

92

But you may retreat and reproach me,
Do your best to worst me, yet you'll not fine
My constancy, my life depends, you'll see,
On yours, retract your love and I'll not pine,
For life itself will burn out bringing relief
To my thirst for your attention, no report
Of my addiction shall subsist, no legend mischief
Do to my love which lives on rarer air, I'll deport
All fear from my mind which will not resist
Your inconsistency with hope, the ore I mine
Is in my residue to submit, not to persist
When you fail me but with death myself decline.
Thus I shall more savage be to my parted self, blind
My traces when you another find, I'll not be left behind.

93

So I shall live deriving heart from you
Like a cuckold gelded but stiff with resolve.
For your loving face still seeming love as true
I your lending looks strive to keep, eyes dissolve
Not with tears but behind a curtain of deceit,
Yet no hatred can take root in that smiling pair.
So I shall find no hostile cause, no receipt
For the grief you would me pay if you would bear
Your absences to me; but your heavy moods
Weighed down by seeping sighs more tell the truth
That belies the heaven of your face which fails to brood
As well as your straining thoughts and heart, I'm uncouth
With love for you, savage in my tenderness, I read
You as I read myself and blindly my faith in you I feed.

94

Those who can evil do but do none,
Whose rough binding deceives their content,
Who throw stones into the pool of emotion
Yet remain fixed as ice, show less their intent
And more thus they rise to knock on God's door
As they harbour their power to forestall heaven.
They are masters of their fate, they restore
Merit as a barrage stores water, others leaven
A poorer grain, more gravel than living wheat.
Like summer flowers which summer arraigns
Though their summer be short and less complete
Than this summary note that shows them again,
If their brand inflates with infection, rank decay,
They stink out heaven and make night of day.

95

In your beauty a slow canker does abide
That burns a spot within which shall shame
Your title, blemish that which once was pride,
The quilted sins you enclose are surely to blame.
The lips that tell a story of you to make report
Are mandated to speak with soft innuendoes
The warrant of your acts and secret thoughts
From dry whispers to storming crescendos,
Thus painting your sins as seeds of decay;
But you are their stem and fragrant flower,
You turn at will your beauty's cover, say
Most shocking blasphemy, yet you tower
Over all honest virtue that flails my passion,
This deceitful joy is purgatory to my fashion.

96

Some say you are false, some say true,
But the kiss of beauty on you is such living grace
All falseness in you a sum of virtue does accrue;
You cultivate faults so only shafts of honesty pace
In your demeanour which precious metal transmutes;
Thus you embroider heaven from the tangle of hell,
With that translation, sin you sincerely commute
To lesser punishment, a million pardons you sell
To your dying conscience, turn your admirers away
From the distant part of you that calls out
To ply the vices your similar virtues display.
You whisper their enticements with devout
Endearments, you play with me this fickle sport,
Being mine, by my final fidelity you shall be taught.

97

Absence from you turns me burning into ice,
Winter spreads its rigour over my incubating sight
Thus blotting out time's proper return twice
As fast from summer's day to winter's frozen night.
Fecund autumn does not bring forth its rich increment,
Its fruit in their prime abundance to my fasting taste,
Nor my unseasonable eyes bend, blind and inclement.
An orphan hope is born unfathered, from my heart displaced.
For summer's glory and dragon light upon you wait
With spectral flowers and birds that silent fly
To replenish the empty space you make, but I create
Winter's winter in heart and sense that I crave to die;
Or if I live, I live only to sufficiently mourn
From dawn to dusk and dusk to ragged dawn.

98

Even rampant spring with its prancing play
When sap grows strong and trees recuse the past
With young laughing leaves, all to the season pray
With hearts that sing out with ardent birth now fast
With promise that unfolds an array of colour and light,
Even then not the busy calls of birds nor soft sighs
Of lovers at night nor fragrance of jasmine delight
Me who am absent from the springing summer of your eyes
Which purpose me to the discourse of timely grief.
My lack of you, my inward winters clearly denote,
Time's not generous but of your presence is a thief,
Poisons my vision only you can serve as antidote.
As long as you forfeit yourself from me and keep away
I'm a lost shadow within your departing presence's play.

The shameless violet brazening the sun
I chided for its larceny of your scent,
This supposed shrinking flower has spun
The air with your sweet amnesty, bent
On dyeing itself with blood set in your cheeks.
The lily too I discompose for it competes
With the satin white of your hand, marjoram seeks
To outshine your hair, but it does not meet
Your hue, and roses too, both red and white,
Blush the one, the other blind, with their median sister
Who pilfers from both, steals your breath from my sight,
And for her theft gluttonous canker cannot resist her
And feeds upon her pride to kill with its fatal bite.
These delinquent flowers I accuse are but a few
Of many that steal their feted beauty from you.

Where is inspiration, the floating angel feather
That tickles words to bring you life?
Does it go on leave for another design together
With its shaman ways that carve like a knife?
Return, fly back gentle muse, redeem
With magus words embers of my delight.
Sing to me who with submissive head esteem
The fury you would breathe into me, your flight
Is my hope again to live through ink and pen
In my love's humour, discover the face I desire,
As new as the day I found it next to mine when
Our hearts were laid side by side and set on fire.
Visitor, root my words deep into my love's fame
So heartless time can neither mark nor surely tame.

Where are you hidden, muse, I would you school
To speak unsalted truth and to season beauty?
You know that truth and beauty on me depend, fools
May say differently, but silence is not your duty's
Friend, you may defend your absence by argument
That truth is truth and needs no eloquence that is sand,
Nor beauty can be laid on pages whose integument
Is already bland so none can contain that which hand
Can create with truth and such beauty which I behold.
None, you say; your riding excuses will not do
For you have in you the secret that me embolds
To speak with hand the truth and beauty I find anew,
So unlock yourself and appear, muse, I'll teach you how
To establish truth, make beauty smile, take future now.

102

My love has bonded with silence, to be still
Is to be steadfast through modest reflection.
I am a pool that is deep and clear, my will
Remains betrothed to you not by easy deflection.
I do not love less because less gloss I apply,
That shine of words and loud avowals which make
Love a pitched commodity in abundant supply.
When love was young I was ready to burn at the stake
And all for show I measured by bravado; now I proceed
More soberly binding passion to counsel, more clear
Less wild the dance, less impetuous blood, I concede;
But no less drawn to you and with purpose dear
And dearer still to the spring of you and me
Where we are eternally young and wish to be.

103

My muse is a beggar when you it describes
That having your plenty before my eyes,
She picks on rags and dull facets subscribes
Creating nothing better than that I despise.
Do not blame me if the poverty I write
Is dross when in the glass you see your face,
My muse is dumb, cannot rise to your heights,
She stutters her brief and withdraws in disgrace.
Be compassionate then with my halting disease,
To be silent is better than to mar with speech,
Yet my verses aspire to your heaven you to please,
Thus your sovereign pardon they do beseech.
I know you more much more than they can say
They are too polite to stay the beauty you display.

104

In my requesting gaze your beauty is still,
My eye meets yours and sees no change,
Your beauty is your age's summoning will,
And summer by winter's course exchanged,
Spring deplete itself through summer's way
To autumn three times since we first met,
Make no inroads in you, I do not quite say
That what I see in you is certain, time frets
Its infinitesimals that creep from edge to edge,
And yet your youth stays me, thus decreed
Is your energy that takes from me the wedge
Of reluctance to love you not with unnatural speed
But seasoned slowness, the luxury of finding you young,
And keep you so with the wit of my embroidering tongue.

105

I worship no idols, no wooden thing
None when I write of you and sing
My words in verse, strive to bring
Your image to life so all who read
Shall see you as you are: virtue
Is your nature, virtue your every deed,
Fair, kind and true, these do not hurt you
But grace you and in turn enliven me.
I cannot speak but of you compose
Verse your constancy to praise, I see
Nothing but good through it imposed
On you which by your beauty raise.
Fair, kind and true you dialect into your only one,
With these ingredients you make radiant the sun.

When I consider and divine from this verse
That lost time that hosted me, it comes down
To listing your beauty's ghosting parts, terse
With speech attached yet joy to conceive, sown
By the poet's wit for my imagination's employ,
When these antique words describe, lip and brow
Unruffled, a pool mirrored by glass, when they deploy
Rhetoric's fashion beauty to conjure and prophesy how
Your state would revive me into being so I can see,
Then with faithful eye, I scan these holy words
To move my wit and receive your loveliness willingly,
So my longing from these lines shall fly to you like a bird.
Your beauty tears me into life thus my love to display,
Passion with my tongue's silence your beauty shall pray.

Neither my fears nor the threshold of the world's unwinding
That fractions the mind and heart with the stamp of night
Can stop you from your rightful place, your beauty's shining
Is a grace to itself beyond control, and to me; you suffer no slight
From the body's predicted parching decline, even the moon
Grows large and small by degrees thus marking time's slumber,
Its vagaries are brought into line by memory in verse that soon
Becomes later, and later soon, and infinity does not encumber
Your light and dark reversed which like the moon grows and wanes.
You are my imagination's cream, your touch and eye alive
In word and sound that escape me on several secret planes.
Fatality does not claim your looks which these gazing lines contrive,
They shall charm time, and recall our joy with their measurement
When time has passed us by, our loving selves being used and spent.

To let my ranging thoughts that strain this page
From my cloistered mind a world materialise
With common characters your privilege
To awe me into speech, but then I realise
Nothing new to refresh this love that spills
Its fire like the springing sun at dawn in you.
Yet I must repeat myself to your *once*, until
I am spent with bending words, if I but knew
A keener scent to spell your hallowed name,
I'd make it my affair so no sly duplicate can lie
With the slant of my voice and pen, without shame
I would act to draw eternal love from its shy
Beginnings and recognise you afresh, ignore your age
Make time swear you young again to run on this page.

Never think me false nor my absence say
Makes me false to you, I'm tied by heart
And soul to your heart and form, cliches
They are, we know, but true; being apart
From your counting eyes for me is to believe
My soul is lost from you, I am laid out so
My absence is false to itself, I would grieve
Its seeming presence in you from whom flow
All that is good in me; I am away from you
Only to return refreshed with love not exchanged
By time's delay, no, I remain constant, true
To my beginning in you with my being constrained
To let your sovereign will in me, for you are my all
You are the afflicted rose in paradise in which I fall.

I know, I know it's true I've fooled about
With you in covert places where motley new
My eyes sharpened my appetite, desires shout
Anew as they repeat an old refrain through
Loving you too lightly and debase, I second
My untrue self when I sail into fresh ports
That entice and withdraw me from you, I reckon
With the felony of changes by which I'm brought
To another youth charging age for golden age.
Yet all they do is prove your embodiment the best;
Now I am done, I've drossed my act, left the stage,
My eyes no longer charm me away, by you they're blest.
So let me in, allow my malfeasance of past releases,
In kissing you I kiss the rest, thus my constancy increases.

111

We cannot speak of gods or goddesses today,
Yet we say fate is always there to take the blame.
So you should chide no one else if you must, the way
Fate played me a lying hand thus, it shames
My name which runs to hide in the public ear
And eye that crowds much more, enough I hope
To forget my deeds which nature blinds, it's clear
I am not debauched yet guilty too, I would elope
With my conscience that serves me pitch, a dish
That deserves my appetite; teach me to breathe again
And I'll absorb your medicine I swear, I will wish
So much to be cured, I shall the heavens attain.
And so I wish you would pity me if you can,
Your compassion augured shall make me a man.

To speak of love and pity from the world
Is to fornicate with truth, but the scroll
Of pity and love's gentle solecism, not hurled
But writ by you on my reputation enrols
My good away from the cast of public derision.
You are like air to me, without you I'm undone,
Without ground to stand on, your eyes envision
My reeling soul so to bring out grace that's begun
By your nurture, then I care not for the whims
Of the world which measure me with haughty looks
That mark the artifice of my powdered name, grim
Reapers of tales, they spoil my brew like too many cooks.
I am so cleanly purposed by your case for me,
That when you speak then with good I shall be.

The morning air, the dreams that close, the songs
That open the day, are felt and seen and heard
By my mind's soliloquy not as they are, strong
Images they may be, but not of themselves, bird
And sea, the fertile oceans that monsters keep,
The rubric of a thousand faces that fashion the day
Devise more than they naturally display, steep
My eyes that seeming see them all within the play
Of the life their teeming apparel heaps on me,
But I am saturated with you who all their forms take
Making me deaf when I hear, blind when I see,
All these awesome or gentle unfolded things forsake
Nature's formal show, estrange my drifted sense
With you who breathe all, wear all, all dispense.

114

Being drunk with you my mind aspires
To crown every jot that busies it with you,
You are its ruler and eye; shadow retires
From your light to dark beyond and through
Any chance of retrieval, your love dethrones
Fear and ugly semblance, base is made gold
By its chemistry which registers me sown
With seeds of your rooting passion, I am bold
Now to convert the bad into better then to best
With your beauty's appetite that in my heart
Grows to make me chaste with eyes undressed
That read my aspect in your unclouded chart
Which dwells in me as prayer dwells in heaven,
I am dough to your salted will that is my leaven.

Perfection is a complaisant word
Too heavy with its own virtue, soft
On its future's offerings that stirred
Me to write in you, look in and so aloft
See clouds for gods where I would judge
Only from that past's present which shows
Prudence for perfection's lie, I grudge
No one to speak an ideal word but you *are* so.
Time's crowding conspiracies replace me with me
So why should I not say now I love you best
And now another perfect best that I blindly see?
Your sovereign present discord is the rest.
So love is flexible it suffers perfection to grow,
I restore with my love your geometry's dearest
With the heart which wants perfection to bestow.

116

Love is not to be conjured with words
It does not dip with time, it's not quicksand
Which swallows all, makes null, neither heard
Nor seen but in the crux of its passing hand.
True love is as constant as the north star,
It reckons time for what it's worth and more
Passing each station intact, age does not mar
Love's suppliant complaint, love is sure
Though time starves out its original goal,
It does not wear a threadbare look.
When assailed by fate's assumptions, it is the pole
Of constancy, its aim is true, it does not brook
Denying change and decay but soars above the hour,
It lives beyond these words that want you to flower.

You may accuse me of truancy
For I am seen to wantonly stray
From your possession with the fluency
Of a philanderer whose attentive sway
Is accounted for by another dress, another step
When I should have been moored to you.
Yes, I have paid address to other minds, kept
Vigil in unmapped places not as true
As the stations of your beginning and end.
I have sailed on different seas
Embedded myself on soil that did not blend
Me with your patient constancy.
But I do appeal to your fierce compassion
To judge me, for I love you in my fashion.

As with flecks of poison I make strong
My taste to speculate a wild reprise
Of impurity as I pluck on pleasure, long
Pains endure to inoculate against fatal disease,
Being full of your patent goodness fierce
With its capture of me; yes I seek to sin
With new authenticity, I am so pierced
With plagues that I do all the more begin
To record your virtue with ills to be cured.
I crave a fabrication of antidotes that shall purge
Me of love of you, from you to be immured.
I replace your gracious song with a choking dirge,
But all estrangement is in vain, for this is true:
My seeking heart is made unripe with absence of you.

With my ailing benefits pollarded that make
Me seem bereft when I am oiled by such
Sin from you, I claim fears that forsake
Hope and turn it still and hope then much
Deploys new franchises to mark my way.
But this is no straight path to read
Sermons from, I am a distracted, prey
To your summons fit for eyes that feed
And wheel all ill the better to cite new curses
That seal the flow from love cut out;
I am consequential now this assign disburses
My winning losses to the four points, the rout
Of my unsighted disgrace, and so I am bent
On you through ills with which I'm spent.

I treat your former harshness as meat
For my own response that diseases me,
My sorrow then is branded so still I treat
With bruised apology, and if the humble fee
Of your disclaimer is to suffer by mine,
Then you, too, have burned through mutual hell.
Even as my distraction takes this hell to refine
My pain for supposed memory's sake, time tells
Another passing and strange reasons makes for acts
That intend us to unripen ourselves, with words keep
Our promises of anger as pocket change, for facts
No longer matter, that's how hard true sorrow sleeps.
But now to our flesh crosses we do sincerely pin
And rescind our deepest sense to keep compassion in.

We wear virtue as our suits or so
We're viewed, for virtue is as it's seems.
I would vice my acts, let virtue go
Since we're judged by what we're deemed
As virtue in our hearts but what with spite
Another wants to steal with poisoned eye.
I would what I am and in my acts find delight,
Nor accountable be to those who would rather die
Than praise true worth or will than their own.
Yet I can make an honest cut and fit, deny
No good deed that access to virtue's throne
If esteem is made virtuous to me, then I'd try
To live as virtue's brief, letting caged virtue free
To be as true as they are true to the vice they see.

122

Your gifted notes do press in me
All your dappled honesty, they rank
Above all determined things that strive to be
In heart and dimpled brain, selves which bank
Your bond that works eternity, till they too
Are absorbed in oblivion's ink to yield
All your form and content false and true.
I am sober with your cause to think and feel
For I have drunk all parts of you that seem
To fill me endlessly, I have no need to tap with ink
And pen for you divine my thoughts and dreams
That I am breached with, tabulated to the brink.
To keep a tally of all I know of you and feel
Demeans both you and me, makes false what's real.

For I am as sure as the pure note that sings
Out to raise the sun from its hiding place,
Yet time, in your haste you think you bring
Change to all, to mountains and to the space
In a heart consecrated to loving, but I
Am fortified against you, I know I'm a point
To you who are eternity's patient for you fly
But endlessly to nowhere; yes, you anoint
All beings with death thus teach me to admire
The dearth of ancient things that seem to second you.
Yet whilst you may dispense with me, my desire
Still stands before and I live long enough to accrue
My dust with the love for which I'm graced,
So by love beyond your call shall I be traced.

If my love were the sliver of capricious time
Spinning here and there, appeasing fame discarding shame,
Thus building my love into a golden calf, no rhyme
Nor reason but eel-like opportunity having claim
On its loyalty, it would be a bastard show
Subject to praise or blame coming from busy lips
That would compress my love with unfettered blows.
But it suffers not from the fetish of anxious regard, slips
Of whispers that court with sly, infamous claims
That bend the throw of my love's straining rubric; it fears
Not these worming policies that would fabricate my aim.
Warped by suspicion, enslaved to the toll of tears,
My love is endeared and untroubled by sights uncouth,
Politic too from use, it sifts these gravid lies from truth.

125

Of course I bring to you my simple fare,
No compound binds my body and soul,
My love is life-bound, pedigreed by care
And grace which flies from eyes with bold
Surmise in loving you; I have seen (I question
Not my own perception) lovers bend to form
And favor fashion's passing deceptions,
Than find the star to steady the peculiar storms
That in their ice rage, then sweetly savour
Simplicity that is the stamp of a loving kiss.
I am not a lover blended with ranked favor
Whose darling affections are hit and miss.
Do not reckon me with measuring eyes
For this soul professes you until she dies.

Time does not dirty your hands nor face
You with timely lines, you hold back
With nature's ardour time whose pace
No mere mortal can retire, time's on track
But you on your way travel back lacking time.
You show your lover's autumn eyes still
Loving you by your timeless bounty that shines
On all of us who journey on without your skill.
You are nature's child who with her cycle defeats
The hours and years with steady death and birth,
Yet trust not youth's short lease, you may repeat
Yourself evenly but your creaturely being to earth
Shall decease and I shall meet you there
Who with you will time's eternity bear.

127

Colours have no bearing, no branded name
To stamp beauty with, yet we know
That fair with beauty duly was acclaimed,
And black was black which beauty didn't show.
But now the world's turned upside down
And black with beauty's grasp is pressing heir
Extracting fair with artfully managed frowns
From the eider of beauty's feinting care,
Beauty is without foreclosure now, a place
To own that surely primes with dutiful
Art that beauty which without disgrace
Calls black fair, thus my lover's eyes are beautiful,
Black tribunes of all the loveliness she assumes,
So my desire for her black with beauty blooms.

128

Honey and milk are not sweet enough nor as good
As that music your fingers bind to ease the air.
I would my lips be numbered so by you should
You symbolise me with those eyes that bear
My risen sun with their speaking, fresh into life.
Strings take heart from your hands with song
That drifts my ear, cuts me with inward strife
From the quick of your parts that belong
Rightfully to these lips which crave to draw
Their potential sap, their soft infections testify
Their craft to your tendered neck and restore
My rapt music which only music can qualify;
If you want to pluck the air that comes from me
Where it will, stroke again and let my coming be.

Do not treacle me with love when lust
Has raised me, this savage god, this devil's cross
Possesses what it sees but never on trust.
No sooner it has its will, that's always another loss,
It grows a thousand-fold with quickening pace;
It pants for possession, ranks reason as a toy,
Compresses the soul to a point without place
Concentrated in the disgrace it employs
To make a monsoon of lovers that reaps
Their breath away casting out their desire's
Enfolding light from its way; so rising lust keeps
Itself to itself thus feeds its appetite and expires
For a while, but like a river's mud that stinks the shore
Lust is ready to rise and sink its prey, then ask for more.

130

Beware of false compassion, a rose is a rose
An eye an eye, no hidden world to conjure there;
My mistress here is absolute, no pickled pose
Can dare her freckled cheek quite compare.
Why even the fretful sun may rise and faltering set
Like her halted breasts but never quite the same.
A division lies between what I see and what abets
My seeing twice her as different speckled selves, lame
As false spring, untrustworthy as bending light
Through water, and her voice, that song of earth
That draws me to my rooted ache, a raucous flight
Of crows may not repeat, like a goddess she gives birth
To my love's stout imagination that cracks night with day,
My mistress is surely beauty yes, but in *her* own way.

I only know your lucid night as tyrannous day,
Yet others more lent to lies can reap a truth
That looks at you and ponders your night and say,
But this is cloud not pellucid light foresooth.
Yet to my crumbling service where heart mind
Replaces, I see fair for cruel, your lambent revelation
Which teaches my soul, duns my spirit, leaves behind
All green doubts that pepper the distillation
Of care I have for you, when resting on another's neck
I weep for thought of you and dowse her skin;
Your black is beautiful and with sure touch wrecks
My judging wit, before you my eyes grow dim;
Yet this I know: though grim in deeds you are
No painted slander mine can your beauty mar.

132

Your eyes are pearls that bind more than show,
Their beauty black becomes mourning to be
The uncovered object of what I want to know
As their sweet accord, for they store me
With past remembered things, though I'm as fresh
With love escrowed for you as on the first day.
And so to speak with several eloquence that mesh
Your disclaiming heart which with torments plays
My part, if it would learn pity from your eyes
That crown the mourning dusk of your face,
Your heart would learn to echo love than to despise
The subject of your sovereign lights that trace
The still flame of love, I will rejoice and start
To live by your eyes better than by your heart.

You divide my friend from me, tear apart
What should be one, deliver dissension where
Dissension has no right, you wound us in the heart
Which pumps for us both, why should we share
Your torture when solitary I would suffice?
Your cruel eye puts a mirror between me and mine
And makes both your creatures slaves, he your device
Hard engrossed in pleasing you who intertwine
Our suffering with the paw of your pleasure.
Cage my love with my will but let his alone,
Reap him if you must, let *me* be your measure,
Now as his own he'll please you, with me atone
With lineaments mine that lie pent in you,
I know we three as one shall come through.

134

I will own to all that you have him whole
And since I'm his, dissolved, I follow too, loaned
To you a parcel for your parts, my soul
Is his thus mortgaged by you, I do moan
With his pain and pleasure who is other mine,
You prison him as he would your prisoner be,
A calibre of dust you raise at will, fine
Actor he is, his theatrical play I attend, you see
As your own, but he lives with me too, still
Wanting you under the lime of your regard.
You have him and me, you may keep or kill
Us as your whim, you may forward or retard
Our distinction with you as one for I'm nothing now he
Is yours and you his chosen meet for mingling you with me.

Your will is bountiful as sultry rain,
You will my own into being that shakes
And marks me to will you in turn from pain.
Yet will you accept me for your will to take?
Is the time that reads me well, far from doubt,
Food to fill your appetite and rub against my will?
Your will is the testament with which you rout
The consideration you wittingly take and instill
With Epicurean zeal in me; I benefit most
When my will and yours fuse into light together,
You are rich with others' good opinions along
The line of your will which stocks and tethers
Bucking mine that scales the wall of our wrong
And right, I am at your will, your passport still
That, potent, would right with you to take my fill.

I will not play this game that needs
A part of me to epitomise and wear
Out my will, I depend on you, seed
Of my love who ripen me with fear
That you may will another to that treasure
That's picked and filled by my ecstatic will.
Oh yes, I will many times come and measure
By instalments your receipt of me, I'll bill
With sighing numbers that accrue in you
Several times by one who holds you so,
For nothing holds me fast but what I do
And say, so you will let me come and go,
And I my parts will install to remedy your ache
Make love to you that will my risen name make.

Though my fool is one-eyed and gross, he charms me
To reflect with eyes that enchant what I see from naught,
They form what he wills, they are encumbered to be
Bewildered by you, sequestered with desire, caught
By your seduction which through your varnish, looks
Before many have singled your supply, tried to be supple
And with suave success, swarming you with timely hooks;
I would swear that you are rarely true since you are coupled
With a thousand heresies of love that with carnival baits
Me whilst others take, then deny you savagely, my eyes
Dreaming this, say *it is not*, with this lie they create
New sciences to tie me down to your plot that me deprives;
My heart and amateur eyes have not served me well
Instead they draw me still to you who surely rifles hell.

138

I know what you are even as you lie
With me whose lies lip themselves on you.
Your truest words rut with lies, you tie
My trust as lovers must by seeming true,
But you and I know we try to live by
Each other's dreaming dark that speaks of light.
So we are poorer through what we give by
Our mounting wills, warping our unequal sight.
Thus we freeze and frame our seeming trust
Hearing what we wish to hear, with truth to bear
What we've done and brought to lie in dust.
Then alone we're found by visiting truth where
Truth does not spare the lies that would deny
The mystery that, through love, learns how to die.

The storm of words I can abide but your look,
That fierce eagle that swoops to beak me,
You may keep for other game, pray brook
Your cause for cruelty which breaks me
With caustic pain, it has no subtle blend
To serve your disdain that puts me down,
I am too simple for such courted gestures that send
Me piece by piece to cold purgatory with a frown
From your burning opals which have bound my soul,
And therefore with the clouded mineral of your eyes
You shall leach the essence my body enrolls,
Thus remove your look, indict me with the spies
Of words that broke their hail into my heart,
But if by your look I'm to be done, I'll pray before you start.

140

Wisdom is a severe cause but not cruel, press
Not my patience to intersperse me with speech
That must be wild and hardly ripe to express
But leaking acid of you, through my pain's reach
Might I presume to teach you to suffer a grain
Of clemency, if not for me, than seeing how I fall
When I'm kneed by your cruelty's edge; I can explain
Nothing as mortal to my frail regard as your call
Upon me, I ask you to be a doctor at my demise,
Remedy with truthful words gentle to my anguish,
But I lose all hope to read you else and to surprise
The better parts of you and me to life, distinguish
The good lodged in you from the bad lest I shall die
Fixed by your heart, than nursed to life by your eye.

My eyes are not your champions, they define
Coldly a face eating youth, limbs whose shape
Is under siege, my nose is no ally of yours, escape
It schemes from your pungent vinegar and wine,
Nor my ears that strain to cope with your voice,
Its morning croak, its evening sibilants, my tongue declines
To speak more honestly of you nor taste too often, choice
Is my senses' incipient rebellion; nor my wits, fine
With thought and imagination that mine love's gold,
Speak so well of you, these addicts delight and shine
In the beautiful only, so easy to please, they're cold,
Apart from my heart, the one thing of mine that you refines.
So I do not skin your various beauty found rancid by my eyes,
I behold it instead with my heart that all foul commentary defies.

142

I would love as I sin and sin as I love,
So much love I have for you whose sin
Is for me an excess of love which proves
You strong with sinful loving that's kin
To my own loving sins which merit yours.
You cannot reprove my sin for saying so,
I only mouth what you do behind doors
In others' beds, yet for my love hate flows
From your virtue, you're pinioned to your mind
That rates me beyond the pale, do not indict
Me with those lips who have stolen as they find,
No more than mine but no less, so do not recite
The litany of my loves you seek as sin in me,
Such faults subscribe you by their own decree.

As a mother sets down her child to chase
After the cat which escapes the front door,
You place me aside become an absent face
For more urgent leys to the attention you store,
Lucid with others' lines you're stolen from me
When you pursue what you think you've lost;
I follow your trace, your image now is conceived
In my imagination's rig that is about to cross
The river of our parting in search of you,
Hoping for your return when you've hunted your goal.
Your memory is oblivion's fetter that hobbles me true,
Now I wait for the rekindling to revive my soul.
So I pray that your absence from itself shall retract,
Then you will return with your absent love intact.

Are my loves outside me or lodged within?
They are like the sun and the moon,
Night and day, one is virtue, the other sin;
Opposing as good and bad they live, yet they'd soon
Die if they were to cease their battle and pure good
Was victorious in my mind and heart; fair
And dark each my loves should be, but could
Bad kill good a desert would bloom there
As fair is rocked by fair ascending deflected dark,
But I am the ring in which fair dark fights,
This devil and angel who my spirit show stark,
They share a common yeast under my skin and sight.
I will never know their balance in my head
Until the one smokes the other out and I'm left for dead.

Your shaping lips, those printed frames for words
That figure thought and fissure feelings, said: *I hate*,
To me who tames impatience and like a fledgling bird
On the tip of flight shivers to hear your real state
Disclose itself, reversing your tone when you see my face –
The staved smile, eyes tuned to your music - the tenacity
My only calling that anchors me on the edge of space,
Receives through your hesitation a glimmer of veracity
From your rationed speech, and you repeal the unsaid
Brimming with silence that, like wax, you preserves;
You open the gates of tender regard reflecting in your head
For when I'm gone, or else you'll have nothing to conserve;
Now you say: *I hate the dust which lies in you and darkens us,*
But I love the love you have to give, that I've learnt to trust.

Your span is surface-bound dust and short,
Undo your brand, dissolve the paint and show,
Your apparel - soul - is light not dross taught
By others' lusts, your gross vanity knows
Nothing but the prison in which you're caught.
Why do you the short time your life spend
With inert diversion like a passion fraught
And drowning on air? Is this all you pretend?
Learn, soul, from the heart's memory that sought
To remove the varnish of your surface, to open it up,
Let light pour in to foster you, be wrought
By your simple spirit singing free, cup
Yourself and feed on life that sustains all of us,
Death plans its rising but live, oh so lightly, as you must.

147

What course have I but to see myself mad,
For in loving you I love not jaunty reason!
I am rhetorical with despair, duly had
By your cold rabble looks which I swear with treason
Against my sinking sense, are warm as the sun
Rising from pure snow, from this fractured knowing
Reason rebels, taking a hard line, regroups
Away from my lunacy alive and growing
With the swish and sway of whims that loop
My distempered heart no physic now can cure,
Nor my mind, slipped from its lock, that words like flies
Besiege, I am determined by you to be frantic and insecure,
At risk from truth's skin that's high with lies
Which swear you are the epitome of all that's fair,
But I speak as a madman his fury, with nothing to declare.

148

What does it mean to see when
All seeing is perplexed, the object
Seen is but a spinning coin, then
Changed from the heart, I'm a subject
When I see you, my eyes weighted
With tears of joy then abject pain;
You my object subject me who is fated
To see obliquely, conceived by my brain.
So how can I discern good from bad
If my eyes are branded never to see right,
How you *are*, how you frown when glad?
I am all I think you want me to be, I delight
In my error that sees your dark moods as benign,
I set my eyes clearly to see as if they were blind.

You find it too easy me to declaim
Saying *I do not love you*, when I lose
My better part in finding you, acclaim
Instead my lapping fidelity for I use
Myself against the grain, tack that gale
To sail near to you; I quickly with anger make
Hard my heart against your enemies who hail
You with false smiles, I do not forsake
You when your name is defamed, I never fail
To quake when you frown and press me down
With the storm of your eyes under which I flail.
My pride is always ready to take a fall, make ground
To love you more than the rumours of your mind,
And I shall love you still even as you are unkind.

I am captured by you, your grazing look
That speaks not of love but smooth disdain
Cuts me not but strings my tune, plucks
My sight, sharpens my taste, I'm inflamed
By your power, my heart's insufficiency bringing
Me close to you, the insolvency of will, defamed
My praise of you since you attune my singing
To the lies you engender to be by others seen
And marked by my capture as the doors
That open to ripen my good, though you demean
By your carving smile that capons me, abhors
What my love plies even as you pause
To spit on my soul, you need none of my applause,
Yet I am your dogged fool married to my cause.

You are a maze in which I lose and find
Myself through that conscience I know
Well of you which me so deeply assigns,
Consciousness instantly traded by your slow
Poison dearly sweet to my growing fault,
The only one that lies in you whole and alert
At your body's call neither lame nor halt,
Ready and in step, salted honey below, to skirt
The treason of my soul, but you with your site
Unveiled magnifies mine to reach your side,
I can only stop to point and touch you right
At your centred display to discover you inside;
Want of you makes me keener, fasting still,
It quickens my part to rise in you and distil.

152

I love you as I love the lies that lie in me,
They make me one with the lying truth you claim
By loving me, you are my sole truthful plenty
That loves me as you break your pledge, you aim
To please me with new faith torn from vows
Not made to me, but nor am I clean with my own
Distracted love for you since I with dark do plough
Another bed and from your field reap the crown
Of all I have to make as scraping oath for your kind
Misuse of me, I swear by this truth your constancy.
And to give you eyes to see I make me blind
So I might patent what I cannot know, instantly
Revealing you as fair and true, thus blaspheme I
To feign our love as unsullied, and swear a lie.

The elixir of life we all seek or so we say,
Stories of Cupid whose art works fire
To love vexed from water and stone, sways
Light against dark where shadows aspire
To keep love in place out of passion's way, girls
May drench themselves with this magus flame,
Young men too, make pith of instincts that whirl,
Coalesce the particles of each thing they name
Like new petty Adams; I would cure my ill
As easily as they if it were not for your sake
Who enthralls me with your gaze that spills
It's brand with unfurling excess in Cupid's wake.
I am limpid only when your smiling eye descends
To fire me more deeply than any knows or pretends.

154

Cupid slept and by his side lay his brand,
A hundred virgins danced by, cool and light,
But one, the fairest, with a discerning hand
Took up the fire that would a million hearts delight
With passion's scorching decree, so disarmed
The folded god dreaming love whose sleep
Was proof that he too could be performed
By an orient world not his own, the maiden leaped
From his sleeping form quick as a doe on heat,
She dowsed the dancing fire in a moonlit pool
Making day its water warmed and complete
With the god's desire which all lovers rules.
Thus love's flame may change in form and attire
Yet it never dies but continues as the living fire.

Finis